HOLYHABITS BIBLE REFLECTIONS | EATING TOGETHER

The Bible Reading Fellowship
15 The Chambers, Vineyard
Abingdon OX14 3FE
brf.org.uk

The Bible Reading Fellowship (BRF) is a Registered Charity (233280)

ISBN 978 0 85746 831 4
First published 2019
10 9 8 7 6 5 4 3 2 1 0
All rights reserved

Text © individual authors 2019
This edition © The Bible Reading Fellowship 2019
Original design by morsebrowndesign.co.uk & penguinboy.net

The authors assert the moral right to be identified as the authors
of this work

Acknowledgements
Scripture quotations marked NIV are taken from The Holy Bible, New
International Version (Anglicised edition) copyright © 1979, 1984, 2011 by
Biblica. Used by permission of Hodder & Stoughton Publishers, a Hachette
UK company. All rights reserved. 'NIV' is a registered trademark of Biblica.
UK trademark number 1448790.

Scripture quotations marked NRSV are taken from The New Revised
Standard Version of the Bible, Anglicised edition, copyright © 1989, 1995 by
the Division of Christian Education of the National Council of the Churches
of Christ in the United States of America. Used by permission. All rights
reserved.

Every effort has been made to trace and contact copyright owners for
material used in this resource. We apologise for any inadvertent omissions
or errors, and would ask those concerned to contact us so that full
acknowledgement can be made in the future.

A catalogue record for this book is available from the British Library

Printed and bound in the UK by Zenith Media NP4 0DQ

EATING TOGETHER

BIBLE REFLECTIONS

40 READINGS AND REFLECTIONS

Edited by
ANDREW ROBERTS

Contents

7 About the writers

8 Introduction to Holy Habits

10 Introduction to Eating Together

Deborah Humphries

12 The blessing of unexpected visitors
Genesis 18:6–10

14 Entertaining angels
Genesis 19:1–3

16 Sharing a feast
Genesis 26:27–31

18 Part of God's family
Genesis 31:51–55

20 Community celebration
Deuteronomy 12:4–7

22 Signs of the kingdom
Ruth 2:13–16

24 God's choices
1 Samuel 9:22–25

26 Justice restored
2 Samuel 9:9–11

28 Trust and obey
1 Kings 17:12–15

30 Plenty for all?
1 Chronicles 29:21–24

Andrew Francis

32 Celebrating together
Nehemiah 8:9–10, 12

34 The Lord is… ?
Psalm 23

36 Called to share
Psalm 36:5–9

Contents

38 The plentiful table helps understand God's wisdom
Proverbs 9:1–6

40 High king of heaven
Isaiah 25:6–9

42 In trust and hope
Isaiah 55:1–3

44 So what should we eat?
Daniel 1:8–12

46 Honouring God
Daniel 5:1–4

48 A call to discipleship
Amos 6:4–6

50 A question of fasting
Matthew 9:14–17

52 Playing by the rules?
Matthew 12:1–2, 6, 8

54 Mission impossible?
Matthew 14:16–20

56 Betrayal
Matthew 26:17, 19–21

58 A dinner party
Mark 2:15–16

60 Rash decisions
Mark 6:21–24, 26

62 Great expectations?
Luke 7:31–34

64 Being vs. doing
Luke 10:38–42

66 Family dinner
Luke 14:12–14

Nell Goddard

Contents

Inderjit Bhogal

68 An open invitation
Luke 14:16–18, 21

70 Sibling rivalry
Luke 15:28–32

72 The healing power of eating together
Luke 19:2–7

74 Eating together – a sign of the kingdom
John 2:7–11

76 Intimate eating
John 6:30–35

78 Sacred meals
John 21:9–13

80 Broadened horizons
Acts 10:11–16, 19–20

82 Body building
Romans 14:14–19

84 Thoughtful eating
1 Corinthians 10:24–31

86 Eating *together*
1 Corinthians 11:17–22

88 Holiness reflected in thankfulness
1 Timothy 4:1–5

90 An open door, an open heart and an open table
Revelation 3:18–22

About the writers

Deborah Humphries is a minister in the Methodist Church who enjoys creative writing. She helped develop the original Holy Habits resources for use in churches in the Birmingham circuit and was part of the team that edited the resources for wider use. She is passionate about growing disciples and building community.

Andrew Francis is a published poet, community theologian, writer and Christian educator. His books include *Hospitality & Community After Christendom* (Paternoster 2012), *What in God's Name Are You Eating?* (Cascade, 2014) and *Eat, Pray, Tell: A relational approach to 21st century mission* (BRF, 2018). He is a retired URC minister, living in a Wiltshire village.

Nell Goddard is a writer at the London Institute for Contemporary Christianity and author of *Musings of a Clergy Child* (BRF, 2017).

Inderjit Bhogal is a theologian and Methodist minister. He is founder and President of City of Sanctuary, a former President of the Methodist Conference and former Leader/CEO of the Corrymeela Community. His work in interfaith relations was recognised with an OBE in the 2005 New Year's Honours list.

Introduction to Holy Habits

> They devoted themselves to the apostles' teaching and fellowship, to the breaking of bread and the prayers. Awe came upon everyone, because many wonders and signs were being done by the apostles. All who believed were together and had all things in common; they would sell their possessions and goods and distribute the proceeds to all, as any had need. Day by day, as they spent much time together in the temple, they broke bread at home and ate their food with glad and generous hearts, praising God and having the goodwill of all the people. And day by day the Lord added to their number those who were being saved.
>
> ACTS 2:42–47 (NRSV)

Holy Habits is a way of forming disciples that is emerging anew from an exploration of this precious portion of scripture, Luke's famous portrait of the early church. As such, it is both deeply biblical and an approach that lives when infused with the life-giving breath of the Holy Spirit – the same Holy Spirit who brought life, energy and creativity to the first Christian communities.

Holy Habits is based upon a series of ten practices that are shown to be fruitful in the Acts 2 passage: biblical teaching, fellowship, breaking bread, prayer, sharing resources, serving, eating together, gladness and generosity, worship, and making more disciples. In this series of material, passages relating to the ten habits are explored one habit at a time, sometimes with reference to other habits. In real life, the habits all get mixed up and complement each other as part of a holistic way of discipleship. You may want to be alert to such connections.

There are many lists in the Bible, and with biblical lists the first and last items often have particular significance. In this list, it is significant that biblical teaching comes first. All of the habits are to be found throughout scripture, and healthy holy habits will be grounded in regular engagement with biblical teaching. This is a foundational habit.

The last habit is also significant. Commentators have remarked that it is no surprise that 'day by day the Lord added to their number' when life was lived in the way Luke describes. Many can be nervous of the word 'evangelism'. Holy Habits offers a way of being evangelistic that may help to assuage some of those nerves.

Holy Habits is a way of life for followers of Jesus individually and collectively. In Acts 2:42–47, Luke offers clues as to how these practices can be fruitful. Note the devotion he mentions at the beginning and the repeated use of the word 'all'. Holy Habits is a way of life for all ages (including children), cultures and contexts. The habits are to be lived day by day, in the whole of life, Monday to Saturday as well as Sunday. And note how Luke attributes the growth that results to the Lord. These are *holy* habits, which flourish when the Lord is at the centre of all.

Introduction to Eating Together

Luke was particularly keen to place food and eating together at the heart of discipleship community. In his gospel, there are 60 references to food and drink and ten occasions in which Jesus is seen sharing a meal. Eating together was a key holy habit of the early church. The word 'together' in the habit title reminds us of the corporate nature of discipleship and the habits that nourish and nurture it. While many of the habits can be practised individually, they all flourish when practised *together*.

The practice of meeting in homes allowed the early Christians to continue the patterns of the table fellowship of Jesus. The atmosphere at the shared meals was one of gladness, and the believers were characterised by their generous, sincere hearts.

People eating together as a sign of God's reign or kingdom goes way back into the Judeo-Christian tradition. It is a picture painted by the prophets and celebrated in the psalms. Jesus was rooted in and lived this tradition. Just as he shared food with all sorts and conditions of people as a sign of the inclusivity of God's kingdom, so too did the early church. The gatherings to eat together were down-to-earth representations of the heavenly banquet imagery that had been reinforced by Jesus through his teaching as well as his actions (Luke 14:14–24). Following in the footsteps of Jesus, the early Christians refused to discriminate against the marginalised. Their table fellowship was characterised by welcome and equality.

The joy of eating together, the value of table fellowship for deepening relationships, the missional fruitfulness of shared meals and the opportunities for sharing faith, biblical study, prayer and worship around the meal table have all been rediscovered in recent years by both new and ancient forms of church. New monasticism places a high value on the sacred experience of eating together. Messy Church has a meal as a key ingredient, as does the most popular evangelism course, Alpha. Café worship at its best integrates worship and food, while Bible study resources have been designed to work around a table sharing food and drink. Churches that work well with students have long realised that the provision of food is a great way to engage with them.

Many of the reflections in this booklet will help you think about how your church can eat together as an act both of fellowship and of mission. As with your reflections on the other holy habits, be attentive to ways in which you can eat together with others at school or work or with your neighbours such that it models the welcome of the kingdom. One other area to be mindful of as we eat together is how our eating impacts creation, for which we have a God-given duty of care. How we eat together today will affect how others can eat together in the future.

| Deborah Humphries

The blessing of unexpected visitors

Genesis 18:6–10

Abraham hastened into the tent to Sarah, and said, 'Make ready quickly three measures of choice flour, knead it, and make cakes.' Abraham ran to the herd, and took a calf, tender and good, and gave it to the servant, who hastened to prepare it. Then he took curds and milk and the calf that he had prepared, and set it before them; and he stood by them under the tree while they ate. They said to him, 'Where is your wife Sarah?' And he said, 'There, in the tent.' Then one said, 'I will surely return to you in due season, and your wife Sarah shall have a son.' And Sarah was listening at the tent entrance behind him.   (NRSV)

| Deborah Humphries

Reflection

Have you ever been surprised by unexpected visitors? I love it when we get a phone call out of the blue from passing friends who want to stop by, because there has been none of the stress of getting the house clean and tidy. The joy of the visit far outweighs my desire for perfection. Whatever is in the fridge or store cupboard is hastily prepared and we enjoy one another's company and catch up around the table. On occasions such as these, I see the true value of eating together.

In today's passage, Abraham and Sarah are rushing around to provide for their guests, offering hospitality according to the customs of their culture. There is attention to detail. Abraham wants to get everything just right. He gives Sarah precise instructions on how to make the cakes – 'choice flour' is to be used – and the calf is 'tender and good'. This may be a surprise visit, but only the best will do. Notice too how Abraham waits beside the men as they eat, just as a servant would, ready to answer to their every need.

We may find it strange that Abraham and Sarah do not eat with their guests, but in the closing verses we realise just how special these visitors really are. They have not met Sarah and yet they know her name and foretell that she will soon give birth to a son.

What matters most when sharing hospitality at home?

Deborah Humphries

Entertaining angels

Genesis 19:1–3

The two angels came to Sodom in the evening, and Lot was sitting in the gateway of Sodom. When Lot saw them, he rose to meet them, and bowed down with his face to the ground. He said, 'Please, my lords, turn aside to your servant's house and spend the night, and wash your feet; then you can rise early and go on your way.' They said, 'No; we will spend the night in the square.' But he urged them strongly; so they turned aside to him and entered his house; and he made them a feast, and baked unleavened bread, and they ate. (NRSV)

| Deborah Humphries

Reflection

I wonder if you have ever entertained angels without realising it.

As two angels enter Sodom, Lot greets them at the city gate. In those days, the gateway was the equivalent of today's town hall, where administration, trade and legal business were conducted. Maybe Lot's working day is ending or maybe he fears for the visitors' safety.

Lot's eager welcome is marked with reverence and respect. He rises to greet the visitors and bows before them, calling them 'my lords' and himself 'your servant'. Perhaps he knows they are angels or perhaps he is simply extending traditional hospitality.

Lot offers overnight shelter and clean feet. Who could resist after travelling along dusty roads in the heat of the day? Lot advises against a night in the square, the city's meeting place. He provides for them 'a feast' accompanied by bread, which is unleavened as he prepares the meal in a hurry.

As I walk through the city centre, I see people living on the streets. Sometimes I give away a cereal bar or coffee voucher; often I walk hurriedly by, embarrassed by my comparative wealth and inadequate response.

I share more than a cereal bar with one man. Perhaps it is the book he is reading that gives me the courage to share common ground; or perhaps, because I take the time to stop, I see the angel within and become the guest at his feast.

> Hospitable God, may we treat everyone we meet
> as a messenger from you.

Deborah Humphries

Sharing a feast

Genesis 26:27–31

Isaac said to them, 'Why have you come to me, seeing that you hate me and have sent me away from you?' They said, 'We see plainly that the Lord has been with you; so we say, let there be an oath between you and us, and let us make a covenant with you so that you will do us no harm, just as we have not touched you and have done to you nothing but good and have sent you away in peace. You are now the blessed of the Lord.' So he made them a feast, and they ate and drank. In the morning they rose early and exchanged oaths; and Isaac set them on their way, and they departed from him in peace. (NRSV)

| Deborah Humphries

Reflection

Prior to this passage, Isaac and his people had been living in Gerar. Abimelech, king of the Philistines, had asked them to move away because they were becoming too powerful. It is understandable, then, that Isaac questions Abimelech's presence. Abimelech, accompanied by his advisor and the commander of his army, wants to make a covenant with Isaac. Perhaps he is afraid that war might break out; certainly, he believes Isaac and his people are 'blessed of the Lord'. In Isaac's time, sealing a covenant with a meal was a sign of friendship, so they share a feast and the next day they exchange oaths.

One of my local churches provides space for Syrian refugees to gather together for mutual support. A group of young Christians from across the city interested in social action wanted to meet with the Syrian young people, so a date was fixed for us to meet them. Imagine our surprise when we were greeted not just by teenagers but by people of all ages. We had come simply to get to know one another, to begin to build relationships, and we were met with an extravagant feast of Syrian food. Although we lacked the language to converse freely, we 'spoke' by eating together and sharing in the generosity of those who had so little. We left knowing that this was the beginning of a beautiful friendship.

> How can food be offered and shared as a way of bringing people together and bridging divides?

Part of God's family

Genesis 31:51–55 (abridged)

Then Laban said to Jacob, 'See this heap and see the pillar, which I have set between you and me. This heap is a witness, and the pillar is a witness, that I will not pass beyond this heap to you, and you will not pass beyond this heap and this pillar to me, for harm'… So Jacob swore by the Fear of his father Isaac, and Jacob offered a sacrifice on the height and called his kinsfolk to eat bread; and they ate bread and tarried all night in the hill country. Early in the morning Laban rose up, and kissed his grandchildren and his daughters and blessed them; then he departed and returned home. (NRSV)

| Deborah Humphries

Reflection

Perhaps you have experienced the pain which follows deception. Not only is trust lost, but relationships can be damaged and often innocent parties get hurt in the crossfire. Somehow, we have to find a way through.

The opening verses of this passage display the uneasy relationship between Jacob and his father-in-law, Laban. Laban tricked Jacob into marrying his eldest daughter. Jacob tricked Laban by the way he made the flocks in his care mate. Both have been guilty of deception, which explains why Laban is so keen to define their territory.

Here, Laban and Jacob overcome their differences and make a covenant. According to custom, the deal is sealed with a sacrifice and a shared meal. The tragic consequence of their falling out is that Laban will no longer see his grandchildren and daughters.

Notice how Jacob turns to God, swearing by 'the Fear' and offering a sacrifice. 'Fear' can also be translated as 'Kinsman', better describing the close relationship between God and Jacob.

When the going gets tough, we too can turn to God, the God who took on human form and seeks to be our kin, to welcome us into God's family. If we can bear to eat with those we have deceived or with those who have deceived us, relationships can be restored. It might take 'all night', but 'in the morning' we might find ourselves blessed.

> Kin-seeking God, give us the courage to try to rebuild broken relationships so that we might all be part of your family.

Deborah Humphries

Community celebration

Deuteronomy 12:4–7

You shall not worship the Lord your God in such ways. But you shall seek the place that the Lord your God will choose out of all your tribes as his habitation to put his name there. You shall go there, bringing there your burnt-offerings and your sacrifices, your tithes and your donations, your votive gifts, your freewill-offerings, and the firstlings of your herds and flocks. And you shall eat there in the presence of the Lord your God, you and your households together, rejoicing in all the undertakings in which the Lord your God has blessed you.   (NRSV)

Reflection

God's people are here being encouraged to keep their faith despite the temptation of the different religions of the people around them. Moses claims Canaan as the place that God has chosen for his people as a centre of worship. The importance of 'the place that the Lord your God will choose... as his habitation' is highlighted throughout Deuteronomy. Perhaps this emphasis on place is particularly significant for a people who are settling in a new land.

God expects the people to go to this special place to perform the rituals and practices of their religion. As they celebrate God's presence and God's blessing, eating together in community is the climax of all that goes before.

Since becoming a minister in north-west Birmingham, I have attended several Caribbean celebrations. Whether honouring a life that has come to an end or a life that is just beginning, an act of worship is often followed by food. The vast array of home-cooked specialities brought by different guests and family members is a way of honouring a person's life and celebrating community. The worship comes first, then the table is blessed before people eat together and share stories of lives past, present and future.

In my experience, a shared meal always has a real sense of gathering in God's presence and rejoicing in God's blessing. As people eat together, community ties are strengthened, and God is given the glory.

How could your community be blessed by preparing food for one another and eating it together?

Deborah Humphries

Signs of the kingdom
Ruth 2:13–16

Then [Ruth] said, 'May I continue to find favour in your sight, my lord, for you have comforted me and spoken kindly to your servant, even though I am not one of your servants.' At mealtime Boaz said to her, 'Come here, and eat some of this bread, and dip your morsel in the sour wine.' So she sat beside the reapers, and he heaped up for her some parched grain. She ate until she was satisfied, and she had some left over. When she got up to glean, Boaz instructed his young men, 'Let her glean even among the standing sheaves, and do not reproach her. You must also pull out some handfuls for her from the bundles, and leave them for her to glean, and do not rebuke her.'

(NRSV)

Reflection

Ruth has gone to the fields to gather the remnants of grain, which the law stated should be left for the alien, the poor, the orphan and the widow.

Boaz acts generously, going above and beyond the letter of the law. He welcomes Ruth at his table and ensures that she has more than enough to eat. He instructs his workers to deliberately leave handfuls of grain behind, in addition to the ears of grain that escape being tied into bundles.

But Boaz is not the only generous one. Ruth has left her home-land and family to accompany her mother-in-law, Naomi, to Beth-lehem, where she then provides for them both. Ruth is grateful to Boaz and treats him with respect, but she does not hold back. Taking her seat alongside the reapers with dignity, she eats until she is satisfied.

All this takes place around the table. Social barriers are broken down as landowner, reapers and gleaners eat together sharing bread and wine: signs of the kingdom.

At our local food bank, clients are offered a drink and as many biscuits as they can eat as they await their food. More important than gifts of food and time is the giving of the self, as around the table, mug in hand, stories are shared, tears are wept and dignity is restored: signs of the kingdom.

> Unpredictable God, give us the grace to receive from unexpected places.

God's choices

1 Samuel 9:22–25

Then Samuel took Saul and his servant-boy and brought them into the hall, and gave them a place at the head of those who had been invited, of whom there were about thirty. And Samuel said to the cook, 'Bring the portion I gave you, the one I asked you to put aside.' The cook took up the thigh and what went with it and set them before Saul. Samuel said, 'See, what was kept is set before you. Eat; for it is set before you at the appointed time, so that you might eat with the guests.' So Saul ate with Samuel that day. When they came down from the shrine into the town, a bed was spread for Saul on the roof, and he lay down to sleep.

(NRSV)

| Deborah Humphries

Reflection

God often confounds our human understanding of worthiness and suitability. Saul has never even heard of Samuel, but Samuel has heard of Saul. God has told him Saul is coming and that he will lead the people of Israel. Saul belongs to 'the least of the tribes of Israel' and the 'humblest' family, yet this is whom God has chosen. Saul and his servant are invited to a special meal and placed at the head of the table. Saul is given the thigh, a cut of meat traditionally reserved for the priest: a subtle indication that Saul has been chosen by God.

God chooses Saul before Saul chooses God. Only after being anointed does Saul acknowledge God. And only then does God give him 'another heart'. Samuel sees beyond Saul's reputation and apparent lack of faith. He listens to God's direction and helps bring Saul to an encounter with God. And where does it all begin? With an invitation to a meal.

Many churches eat together regularly as part of their fellowship. Around the table, friendships are formed, the seeds of faith are sown and disciples are nurtured. I am convinced that the success of discipleship courses that include eating together are as much, if not more, about the conversations around the table than they are about the formal teaching.

Who does God want you to invite to eat with you, and how could you enable them to meet with God?

Deborah Humphries

Justice restored

2 Samuel 9:9–11

Then the king summoned Saul's servant Ziba, and said to him, 'All that belonged to Saul and to all his house I have given to your master's grandson. You and your sons and your servants shall till the land for him, and shall bring in the produce, so that your master's grandson may have food to eat; but your master's grandson Mephibosheth shall always eat at my table.' Now Ziba had fifteen sons and twenty servants. Then Ziba said to the king, 'According to all that my lord the king commands his servant, so your servant will do.' Mephibosheth ate at David's table, like one of the king's sons. (NRSV)

| Deborah Humphries

Reflection

In this passage, King David fulfils the promise he made to Jonathan to take care of his family. Mephibosheth was just five years old when his father died, and now he is a father himself. Either David or Ziba had been benefitting from 'all that belonged to Saul and to all his house'. Now Mephibosheth's inheritance is restored, and Ziba and his sons and servants are to work for him. As a mark of respect, Mephibosheth is invited to eat at the king's table, as great a privilege then as it is today.

We shall never know why it took David so long to restore Mephibosheth's birthright. Perhaps it is only now that David has established his kingship, that he feels able to pay tribute to his beloved friend's son in such a public way.

I wonder which person you relate to in this story.

Is it David, restorer of justice, supporter of the underdog? Do you enjoy inviting people to eat with you at your table?

Or are you like Ziba, obedient servant awaiting instruction from others before doing what you know is right? Are you happier serving others than sharing the table?

Or maybe you are more like Mephibosheth, reluctantly taking your place at the king's table despite your sense of unworthiness.

> God of the table, you invite us to be your guest at every meal. Show us how to eat together in a way that restores justice for all.

Deborah Humphries

Trust and obey

1 Kings 17:12–15

But she said, 'As the Lord your God lives, I have nothing baked, only a handful of meal in a jar, and a little oil in a jug; I am now gathering a couple of sticks, so that I may go home and prepare it for myself and my son, that we may eat it, and die.' Elijah said to her, 'Do not be afraid; go and do as you have said; but first make me a little cake of it and bring it to me, and afterwards make something for yourself and your son. For thus says the Lord the God of Israel: The jar of meal will not be emptied and the jug of oil will not fail until the day that the Lord sends rain on the earth.' She went and did as Elijah said, so that she as well as he and her household ate for many days.

(NRSV)

Reflection

Elijah has told King Ahab that there will be 'neither dew nor rain' (17:1): divine punishment for the nation's idolatry. The fertility god Baal is unable to send much-needed rain and yet the God of Israel provides his prophet with water from the wadi and food brought by ravens.

God sends Elijah to Zarephath, the birthplace of Baal worship. Here, he encounters a widow who acknowledges God as 'the Lord', and Elijah asks for bread and water.

Elijah's request to the widow to cook for him before cooking for her and her son seems incredulous. Elijah reassures her that God will not let the meal or the oil run out. And sure enough, 'she as well as he and her household ate for many days'.

Elijah trusted in God, the widow trusted Elijah and all was well; but I'm left with lots of questions.

How can it be right to ask so much of someone who has so little?

Why did God provide for Elijah and the widow, and yet thousands starve to death every day because of drought and famine?

Perhaps my indignation is wrongly placed. It is not up to me to discern who has the desire or the right to share their resources. Perhaps dignity is restored as people share with glad and generous hearts as they experience the joy of eating together.

> All-knowing God, help us to hear your voice
> and trust your answers.

Deborah Humphries

Plenty for all?

1 Chronicles 29:21–24

On the next day they offered sacrifices and burnt-offerings to the Lord, a thousand bulls, a thousand rams, and a thousand lambs, with their libations, and sacrifices in abundance for all Israel; and they ate and drank before the Lord on that day with great joy. They made David's son Solomon king a second time; they anointed him as the Lord's prince, and Zadok as priest. Then Solomon sat on the throne of the Lord, succeeding his father David as king; he prospered, and all Israel obeyed him. All the leaders and the mighty warriors, and also all the sons of King David, pledged their allegiance to King Solomon. (NRSV)

| Deborah Humphries

Reflection

It's hard to imagine 'a thousand bulls, a thousand rams, and a thousand lambs'. No expense has been spared at this extravagant celebration. Following King David's lead, the people have given generously to rebuild the temple. Coming before God in worship and praise, they offer 'sacrifices and burnt-offerings', eating and drinking 'before the Lord… with great joy'. Solomon is anointed as king and 'the Lord's prince'. The people pledge their loyalty to the new king and a time of prosperity and stability begins.

This story reminds me of a church 'faith' lunch or supper. There might not be a thousand bulls, a thousand rams, and a thousand lambs, but there's always plenty to eat and usually there is 'great joy'. Such a meal might follow a special act of worship where the congregation has presented their offerings to God and given thanks for all that God has provided. Here, the eating together 'before the Lord' highlights a commitment to God and one another as relationships are developed and community is formed.

Yet around the table are the 'usual suspects', and there are people who are missing – members of the worshipping community who never stay. Perhaps you have not advertised the meal adequately or they feel excluded from the 'in crowd'; perhaps they have other commitments or need to get home to friends or family; perhaps they find it difficult to eat in public or cannot afford to bring something to share.

> The next time you eat together as church, think about how you can enable table fellowship for all.

| Andrew Francis

Celebrating together

Nehemiah 8:9–10, 12 (abridged)

Then Nehemiah the governor, Ezra the priest and teacher of the Law, and the Levites who were instructing the people said to them all, 'This day is holy to the Lord your God. Do not mourn or weep.' For all the people had been weeping as they listened to the words of the Law. Nehemiah said, 'Go and enjoy choice food and sweet drinks, and send some to those who have nothing prepared... Do not grieve, for the joy of the Lord is your strength'... Then all the people went away to eat and drink, to send portions of food and to celebrate with great joy, because they now understood the words that had been made known to them.   (NIV)

Reflection

This is an inspirational passage to challenge us. Its background is the narrative of Artaxerxes sending Nehemiah to Jerusalem to oversee the rebuilding of the city. Nehemiah surveys the broken-down walls quietly by night, then calls God's faithful people to act together in the rebuilding. How life-giving is it when the people of God work together for the common good of all the people (whether of faith or not) across a town or city?

The eagle-eyed will notice that I have omitted verse 11 from the quoted NIV text. This was deliberate, as it simply records how the Levites, as the temple servants, affirm like a chorus that this is a sacred day for celebration. How good is it that all the city's religious leaders share the same community message to celebrate the good things that God has set down?

The clear challenge of this passage is in recognising the nature of the celebration. It is inclusive of all – not just those who rebuilt the walls; not just those who listened to the faithful reading of God's word, who wept together at its clarity; not just their households who feasted to celebrate the walls' completion. Even those too poor to have enough or too slothful to prepare food were to receive from others' generosity.

> God's people are still called to rebuild our towns, cities and villages – and celebrate what is done. Whether it is our congregational support of the local food bank, providing a weekly meal at the night shelter or giving consistently of our plenty, we are called to act.

| Andrew Francis

The Lord is...?

Psalm 23

The Lord is my shepherd, I shall not want. He makes me lie down in green pastures; he leads me beside still waters; he restores my soul. He leads me in the rights paths for his name's sake. Even though I walk through the darkest valley, I fear no evil; for you are with me; your rod and your staff – they comfort me. You prepare a table before me in the presence of my enemies; you anoint my head with oil; my cup overflows. Surely goodness and mercy shall follow me all the days of my life, and I shall dwell in the house of the Lord my whole life long.

(NRSV)

Reflection

Several times during my ministry, I have led residential church weekends based upon this psalm. Each of the six sessions took one verse and explored its theme interactively.

As we gathered on the Friday evening, we could easily reflect upon a shepherd's gathering the sheep into the fold. We could rejoice in being away together, be it under canvas or in a conference centre, knowing that we 'shall not want' (v. 1) in our shared meals, laughter, prayer and conversation.

That was echoed in our Saturday morning sessions, where we first recognised God's provision (v. 2) as we shared in Bible study and meal preparation for later. We then reflected upon our back-at-home congregational life and service to others (v. 3).

By Saturday evening, barriers had broken down after afternoon walks and visiting local tea shops. We found we could speak and listen together about the way God has 'comforted' us in times of trial, illness, bereavement and family breakdown. We learned from each other how in God we should 'fear no evil' (v. 4).

Our Sunday morning Communion service focused on how God had 'prepared a table' so that within God's reign there would be bread for all. Within worship, we anointed those who wanted to make a fresh commitment to follow Jesus (v. 5). Our final post-lunch session invited each of us to recognise how God's 'goodness and mercy' (v. 6) always follow us. So we stepped out afresh into 'the house of the Lord', which was now far bigger than the church we came from.

> How and when could you and your church undertake this kind of reflective journey?

| Andrew Francis

Called to share

Psalm 36:5–9

Your steadfast love, O Lord, extends to the heavens, your faithfulness to the clouds. Your righteousness is like the mighty mountains, your judgements are like the great deep; you save humans and animals alike, O Lord. How priceless is your steadfast love, O God! All people may take refuge in the shadow of your wings. They feast on the abundance of your house, and you give them drink from the river of your delights. For with you is the fountain of life; in your light we see light.

(NRSV)

Reflection

Let the poetry and imagery of this passage capture your hearts and minds. It is such an affirmation of God's ongoing provision.

Belief in our God tells of a rich creation, which affirms the strength and size of God's love, faithfulness, righteousness and justice. The psalmist is calling God's faithful people to proclaim and sing of a world where these divine values are daily recognised. How different would our neighbourhoods, natural environments and international politics be, if only the faithful people of God were so united that 'the world' heard that song?

God seeks the best for all the created order. That Hebrew word 'save' ('preserve' in the NIV) contains the sense of 'encouragement to thrive', not simply to exist. Whoever we are, whether the chick of an eagle or a sparrow, we too find our covering in the shadow of God's maternal wings; we are safe when accepting God's overarching and priceless loving presence.

We must learn from the psalmist and the early New Testament church, when rich and poor, powerful and powerless could eat together and be fed. God's abundance is for all – not the few. In our world of plenty, what stops the poor and hungry (both humans and other creatures) drinking from God's overflowing river of delight?

A friend has a 'paradise garden', with shady arbours, many fruit trees and a central trickling but perpetual fountain. In that place, I am reminded of these verses, that the Persian word *paradeiso* means 'a garden of plenty for all' – literally a paradise – where the light of understanding trickles outward from us as we share God's abundance, God's values and God's love.

| Andrew Francis

The plentiful table helps understand God's wisdom

Proverbs 9:1–6

Wisdom has built her house, she has hewn her seven pillars. She has slaughtered her animals, she has mixed her wine, she has also set her table. She has sent out her servant-girls, she calls from the highest places in the town, 'You that are simple, turn in here!' To those without sense she says, 'Come, eat of my bread and drink of the wine I have mixed. Lay aside immaturity, and live, and walk in the way of insight.'   (NRSV)

| Andrew Francis

Reflection

This beautiful narrative call from the book of Proverbs both gives an invitation and sets up a contrast.

In the Hebrew Bible, the person of Wisdom is the inspiration or breath (*ruach*) of God, which enables fuller living and understanding. The New Testament and Christian parallel is the person and work of the Holy Spirit.

The contrast is between those whose lives have been inspired by Wisdom and those who show 'immaturity', who show no understanding of the words, works and ways of God. Wisdom indicts and invites those 'without sense', that is, those without faith. So, our passage ends with a call to leave the 'simple' ways of faithlessness to 'walk in the way of insight'.

But how? In echoes of Psalm 23 (p. 34), those who hear Wisdom's call are invited to share in the bounty and provision of our creator God. The table is spread with rich things. When I ran a retreat house in France, we helped people understand the mixing of wine (with water) to aid digestion, avoid inebriation and keep clear heads for discussion and understanding. We followed Wisdom's practical advice. Our visitors learned of the faith as we sat, ate and talked at the communal table of God's provision.

In my book *Eat, Pray, Tell* (BRF, 2018), I explain how using Jesus' own model of home-based hospitality with meals can lead the 'simple' towards faith-filled dialogue. Wisdom prevails. In offering God's invitation to eat together, others can recognise his provision and inspiration to learn to 'walk in the way of insight'.

> Lord, fill me afresh with your wisdom, I pray.

| Andrew Francis

High king of heaven

Isaiah 25:6–9

> On this mountain the Lord Almighty will prepare a feast of rich food for all peoples, a banquet of aged wine – the best of meats and the finest of wines. On this mountain he will destroy the shroud that enfolds all peoples, the sheet that covers all nations; he will swallow up death for ever. The Sovereign Lord will wipe away the tears from all faces; he will remove his people's disgrace from all the earth. The Lord has spoken. In that day they will say, 'Surely this is our God; we trusted in him, and he saved us. This is the Lord, we trusted in him; let us rejoice and be glad in his salvation.'
>
> (NIV)

| Andrew Francis

Reflection

Several years ago, an Irish Roman Catholic bishop invited me to co-lead an ecumenical pilgrimage up the Hill of Tara, the seat of the ancient high kings of Ireland. It is hardly a mountain, but after a service in the eastern summit-side St Patrick's church, we ate outdoors, all sharing our food. My hosts had brought wine, Guinness, chicken legs and a venison pie in their packed rucksack, to share freely. I remembered this passage as we surveyed the vista of God's grandeur.

The myths, legends and factions of the warring Irish kings were forgotten on Tara's hill of peace, as Protestant and Catholic ate together. Isaiah talks of the deathly 'shroud' (or winding sheet) that 'enfolds all peoples'. But did Isaiah mean the end time, when God will set all things right and there will be no more warring kings, death, pain or suffering? We do know this: Isaiah's vision of God's grandeur is that God will accomplish what he promised – and all tears will be wiped from the faces of a grieving humanity.

The faithful need to recognise God's coming vision, so 'let us rejoice and be glad' in what God is accomplishing. I walked down from the Hill of Tara, the place where warring kings came to talk peace and share food. My heart was humming with Mary Byrne's translation of the ancient Irish hymn 'Be thou my vision', which ends with that visionary verse: 'High king of heaven… after victory is won'. Isaiah tells us why God is ruler of all forever.

What will make your heart hum today? With whom could you eat to make peace?

| Andrew Francis

In trust and hope

Isaiah 55:1–3 (abridged)

'Come, all you who are thirsty, come to the waters; and you who have no money, come, buy and eat!... Why spend money on what is not bread, and your labour on what does not satisfy? Listen, listen to me, and eat what is good, and you will delight in the richest of fare. Give ear and come to me; listen, that you may live. I will make an everlasting covenant with you, my faithful love promised to David.' (NIV)

Reflection

I love this passage. It reminds me of the food cooperative we ran at an inner-city church, and it brings back so many other memories. Our ministry reached far beyond Sunday's congregations to many in the neighbourhood who financially struggled. With every bag of flour sold, we attached a bread recipe and an invitation to bread-making classes. We wanted to enrich the quality of others' lives. In those days before food banks, we often gave food away to those with 'no money'. I have lost count of how many times my heart has sung when I have heard of another inner-city church offering cookery classes so that others learn to 'eat what is good and... delight in the richest of fare'.

Note the repetitive invitations to 'come... come' and to 'listen, listen to' God's prophet. We are the ones who must repeatedly create the welcome, the ones who must share Isaiah's message in practical, everyday ways.

As we heed Isaiah's injunctions and trust in what we can offer in God's name, people will come. The message will be heard by some, perhaps not all. Missional discipleship serves others, enabling them to share 'life to the full' (John 10:10).

When our two pet cats came to us, they were just kittens who had to learn to trust us for their daily food and care. They have rewarded us with trust and love. In them, we learned more of what God means in the declaration, 'I will make an everlasting covenant with you', where love and trust grow from understanding the provision beyond ourselves.

> To whom could you be a blessing and demonstrate God's love by offering cookery classes or something similar? For example, could you work with a local school to help children and young people learn how to cook healthily?

Andrew Francis

So what should we eat?

Daniel 1:8–12

Daniel resolved not to defile himself with the royal food and wine, and he asked the chief official for permission not to defile himself in this way. Now God had caused the official to show favour and compassion to Daniel, but the official told Daniel, 'I am afraid of my lord the king, who has assigned your food and drink. Why should he see you looking worse than the other young men of your age? The king would then have my head because of you.' Daniel then said to the guard whom the chief official had appointed over Daniel, Hananiah, Mishael and Azariah, 'Please test your servants for ten days: give us nothing but vegetables and water to drink.'

(NIV)

Reflection

This is the key exchange in a splendid narrative. The Babylonian king commanded that four enslaved Israelite men from the royal household be trained to become his advisers. They were to be fed from the royal table, receiving rich food and drink. But this would have been an affront to those following Jewish dietary laws, hence Daniel's request for permission to be excused.

Daniel bargains for a simple vegetarian diet with water, rather than rich foods and wines.

The Vegetarian Society's magazine frequently claims that ten per cent of British people are now exclusively or predominantly vegetarian. I am an omnivore, but my partner and daughter are both vegetarians. As a family, we know that eating a good vegetarian diet maintains our health. Increasingly, European research questions the wisdom of eating too much red meat or regularly eating processed meats. Daniel knew something that many people choose to ignore today.

In my book *What in God's Name Are You Eating?* (Cascade, 2014), I explore how Christians should question the everyday diet that our supermarkets and corner shops try to foist upon us. I advocate an increasing simplicity of life and diet; we grow nearly all our summer vegetables and many of our winter ones, too. We live well on organic, simple fare – something Daniel knew too.

This biblical narrative continues with these four vegetarian Israelites subsequently providing some of the best counsel ever to the Babylonian king. They became his most trusted and special advisers. Who said, 'You are what you eat'? Is it time to prayerfully review your diet?

Honouring God

Daniel 5:1–4

> King Belshazzar gave a great banquet for a thousand of his nobles and drank wine with them. While Belshazzar was drinking his wine, he gave orders to bring in the gold and silver goblets that Nebuchadnezzar his father had taken from the temple in Jerusalem, so that the king and his nobles, his wives and his concubines might drink from them. So they brought in the gold goblets that had been taken from the temple of God in Jerusalem, and the king and his nobles, his wives and his concubines drank from them. As they drank the wine, they praised the gods of gold and silver, of bronze, iron, wood and stone. (NIV)

| Andrew Francis

Reflection

Several of my friends have been rewarded for their community service with invitations to a Buckingham Palace garden party. Each returned saying how unostentatious it had been for such a prestigious event. Yes, there was beautiful bone china, but this was used to serve simple but delicious tea, cake and finger food… and yes, the Queen ate the same food as they did.

What a contrast with King Belshazzar, who wanted to show off his wealth, using the spoils of war and oppression. This passage describing the king's excess immediately precedes the moments when a hand appears and writes upon the wall. Of all the king's advisers, only Daniel can translate the words, foretelling the end of that Persian royal dynasty because of their failure to honour God. That very night, Belshazzar is slain and Darius the Mede becomes king.

In their egotism, Belshazzar and his father lost their minds and their lives. The seeds of their downfall were in their love and flaunting of material things – not just gold and silver – as they failed to honour God, who rules over all: 'You shall have no other gods before me' (Exodus 20:3).

Whether we are leaders or followers, we are all servants of Jesus, whose own unostentatious way was that of humility; therefore, this is our calling too.

Is there anything unnecessarily ostentatious in your lifestyle, including the types of food and drink you buy? In what ways could you honour God by living more simply?

A call to discipleship

Amos 6:4–6

You lie on beds adorned with ivory and lounge on your couches. You dine on choice lambs and fattened calves. You strum away on your harps like David and improvise on musical instruments. You drink wine by the bowlful and use the finest lotions, but you do not grieve over the ruin of Joseph.

(NIV)

Reflection

Unlike Julie Andrews in *The Sound of Music*, we will not 'start at the very beginning' but at the end. What is 'the ruin of Joseph'? Every Bible translation and paraphrase is differently nuanced. It is a sting in the tail to remind us of the ruin of Israel, God's chosen, their hurt and affliction in failing to understand the breadth of God's call to them.

All that precedes it is a challenge to our comfort and missional discipleship. One in seven people in the world live below the poverty line and over half of the global population live in cities. Jesus' followers must recognise the gospel's 'bias to the poor' and the challenge of urban mission.

To walk the boardwalks of Klong Toey, Bangkok, or the steep paths of Rocinha, Rio de Janeiro, or Dharavi's streets in Mumbai is eye-opening for western Christians. These are all poorly built, overcrowded slums. To walk them in company with Christian co-workers is revealing. To work alongside them, sleeping on a mat on a shanty town floor is demanding.

Amos needs to challenge Christians in every generation. We are not called to a life of ivoried beds, continual feasting and excessive drinking. Too much meat-eating damages the planet. God's world is becoming 'the ruin of Joseph' through human inequality and the greed of a westernised minority. The vocation and agenda of Christian discipleship is missionary servanthood.

Two friends, Ash and Anji Barker, lead the Newbigin House ministry, in Winson Green, Birmingham, just yards from where Channel 4 filmed the infamous *Benefits Street*. For years, the Barkers worked in Klong Toey. They have let go of earthly comforts to share the 'reign of God', to rebuild ruined lives and to remind the rest of us that prophetic, sacrificial discipleship is possible.

Lord, as I enjoy my food, may I never forget those whose poverty is ruinous.

49

Andrew Francis

A question of fasting

Matthew 9:14–17

Then John's disciples came and asked [Jesus], 'How is it that we and the Pharisees fast often, but your disciples do not fast?' Jesus answered, 'How can the guests of the bridegroom mourn while he is with them? The time will come when the bridegroom will be taken from them; then they will fast. No one sews a patch of unshrunk cloth on an old garment, for the patch will pull away from the garment, making the tear worse. Neither do people pour new wine into old wineskins. If they do, the skins will burst; the wine will run out, and the wineskins will be ruined. No, they pour new wine into new wineskins, and both are preserved.' (NIV)

Andrew Francis

Reflection

The Greek word for fasting means going without food, so for some, fasting had become a way of avoiding 'unclean' food on holy days – a mere ritual.

John the Baptist's disciples were confused when they saw the Pharisees fasting, as they did, while Jesus' followers appeared not to. Previously, Jesus had told his disciples, 'When you fast, do not look sombre as the hypocrites do' (Matthew 6:16). In other words, do not let your fasting be known to others. So should they fast or not?

Jesus takes his teaching further – beyond matters of simple religious observance. Jesus declares himself to be 'the bride-groom' and his earthly ministry akin to a wedding, when people celebrate – not fast. Using everyday Galilean examples, Jesus illustrates that the new ways of the 'reign of God' cannot be constrained by the practices of old-style ritual.

Our Christian tradition uses fasting at times of liturgical preparation (e.g. Advent, Lent) or during retreats to help us physiologically concentrate on prayer, vocation and the task of discernment. This passage encourages us, if we choose to fast, to do so joyfully because the 'kingdom of heaven has come near' (Matthew 3:2). As we celebrate sharing in the words, works and ways of the ever-present Jesus, fasting becomes a way of feasting on the goodness of God and a way of drinking in the new wine of the kingdom.

How might God be calling you to fast? If you choose to fast, please make sure it is medically safe to do so.

| Nell Goddard

Playing by the rules?

Matthew 12:1–2, 6, 8

A t that time Jesus went through the cornfields
on the Sabbath. His disciples were hungry
and began to pick some ears of corn and eat
them. When the Pharisees saw this, they said
to him, 'Look! Your disciples are doing what is
unlawful on the Sabbath'... [He answered,] 'I
tell you that something greater than the temple
is here... For the Son of Man is Lord of the
Sabbath.'

(NIV)

| Neil Goddard

Reflection

Fill in the blank: 'Rules were made to be…'

Followed? Broken? People tend to divide into one of those two camps. The Pharisees in this passage were in the former group. The disciples were seemingly in the latter, as they were breaking the Jewish law by 'reaping' the grain on the sabbath. And so the Pharisees, driven by systems and rules and so keen to obey their interpretation of scripture, condemned the disciples and asked Jesus to do the same.

But Jesus turns things on their head. He puts human need – including the basic human need to eat – over rules and rituals. There's a new system at play now. The game has changed, and so too have the rules and their interpretation. God is at work and, as the Messiah, Jesus is the bringer of the new system: 'Something greater than the temple is here… for the Son of Man is Lord of the Sabbath.' Jesus, God in human form, is more significant than the temple and all its rules and rituals. That's not to say that all of the rules have gone out of the window and it's now a free-for-all. The law still matters. But the message of this passage is simple: with Jesus, compassion trumps ritual. People matter more than rules.

However you feel about rules, this passage brings a challenge: what comes first – in our churches, our homes, our workplaces, our families? The 'way we've always done things' and the rules we've created, or the human needs of those around us?

What would it look like, in your daily life, to elevate Jesus above rules and systems and to his rightful place as Lord of all?

> Father, thank you that Jesus is Lord of the sabbath. Teach me to seek and follow Jesus first above all else – even the rules and systems of the world.

Nell Goddard

Mission impossible?

Matthew 14:16–20

Jesus replied, 'They [the crowds] do not need to go away. You give them something to eat.' 'We have here only five loaves of bread and two fish,' they answered. 'Bring them here to me,' he said. And he told the people to sit down on the grass. Taking the five loaves and the two fish and looking up to heaven, he gave thanks and broke the loaves. Then he gave them to the disciples, and the disciples gave them to the people. They all ate and were satisfied, and the disciples picked up twelve basketfuls of broken pieces that were left over. (NIV)

| Nell Goddard

Reflection

Have you ever been given a seemingly impossible task? A ridiculously short deadline at work or a large group of people to feed at very short notice? If you have, you'll be able to understand a little of what the disciples probably felt here.

The only miracle recorded in all four gospels, this is one of those stories where Jesus' compassion (and concern that people are properly fed) seems to extend beyond the reasonable and into the ridiculous. How could the disciples possibly feed 5,000 men, plus women and children, on five loaves and two fish? It is, without a doubt, an impossible task.

Maybe you have questions like that in your life – how, Jesus, can I possibly do what you're asking of me? Or even, how can I feed my family? Do you not see my limited resources, my lack of time, my difficult family, my rented accommodation, my struggling finances? Why are you asking me to do the impossible?

This story is a reminder that Jesus is not limited by a lack of material provision – or lack of ability or experience or age or qualifications. All he asks of us is the little we can offer, given in humility. He will take it, he will give thanks for it and then he will provide from it.

And when we do that together, there comes unity and community: from five loaves and two fish, we see over 5,000 people sitting, reclining, eating together. From an impossible task to a beautiful scene: all Jesus asks is that we give him the little that we have and trust that he can – and will – do the rest.

> Offer God what little you have today, in faith that he will multiply it and create something beautiful. And if you have a lot, how might you share this to help others eat well?

Nell Goddard

Betrayal

Matthew 26:17, 19–21

On the first day of the Festival of Unleavened Bread, the disciples came to Jesus and asked, 'Where do you want us to make preparations for you to eat the Passover?'... So the disciples did as Jesus had directed them and prepared the Passover. When evening came, Jesus was reclining at the table with the Twelve. And while they were eating, he said, 'Truly I tell you, one of you will betray me.'

(NIV)

Reflection

If you've ever celebrated Passover, you'll know that it involves not just eating and drinking, but telling stories, prayer, worship and physical actions. It is a feast not only for the taste buds, but for the mind as well, as you journey through the history of the Jewish people, celebrating their freedom from bondage in Egypt and God's faithfulness through the years.

It is this meal that Jesus is celebrating before his death; this is how he chooses to spend his final night with his disciples. The fact that Jesus is reclining is important; it is a key part of the Passover feast. Those celebrating together would lean on their left side to accentuate the fact that they are a free people – in ancient times only free people were able to recline while eating.

It seems strange that Jesus is reclining in the presence of the one who he knows will betray him, celebrating freedom in the face of treachery. If you've ever shared a meal with someone who has betrayed you or hurt you deeply, you'll know something of Jesus' pain here. But still he chooses to sit, recline, eat and celebrate freedom with his friends – and his betrayer.

And yet... if Jesus will recline at the table, celebrating freedom and God's faithfulness with the one who would turn him over to the Roman authorities, it is but a foretaste, a glimpse, a glimmer of the way in which he will welcome us – those who have betrayed him also – into the great feast of heaven as we celebrate ultimate freedom and God's eternal faithfulness.

> Bring before God those who have betrayed you or hurt you deeply and with whom you might find it difficult to eat, and pray that you would be able, in his strength, to forgive them.

| Neil Goddard

A dinner party

Mark 2:15–16

> While Jesus was having dinner at Levi's house, many tax collectors and sinners were eating with him and his disciples, for there were many who followed him. When the teachers of the law who were Pharisees saw him eating with the sinners and tax collectors, they asked his disciples: 'Why does he eat with tax collectors and sinners?'
>
> (NIV)

| Nell Goddard

Reflection

If God were to rock up in human form in the 21st century, who do you think he'd choose to hang out with? Where do you think he'd have his meals? If you were to ask the general population, you'd likely receive answers such as 'with the Archbishop of Canterbury' or 'at Buckingham Palace'.

The same was expected of the Messiah in Jesus' day. Many expected him to spend time with the Pharisees and the teachers of the law – the ones who knew the scriptures and had their lives together. They thought he would share meals with those who would say the right things and act in the right way.

But Jesus didn't. He continually astounded the Pharisees by eating with 'tax collectors and sinners' – with societal outcasts, with the despised common people who had no understanding of the law or the scribal tradition. Jesus never ceased to go against expectations, and he called the most unlikely, the most common, the most broken, the most ritually unclean people to come and eat with him.

Jesus broke bread with the outcasts. He invited to the table those who were sinners and whom many thought had no chance of fellowship with God. He turned societal, cultural and religious expectations on their head.

What would it look like for us to do the same? To share our table, our homes and even our lives with those whom others consider to be broken and beyond help? For that is exactly what Jesus did – and what he does with us, welcoming sinners into fellowship with a holy God.

Bring before God those whom the world sees as today's 'tax collectors and sinners', as broken and beyond help. Ask him to show you how to reach out to and love them like he does.

| Nell Goddard

Rash decisions

Mark 6:21–24, 26

On his birthday Herod gave a banquet for his high officials and military commanders and the leading men of Galilee. When the daughter of Herodias came in and danced, she pleased Herod and his dinner guests. The king said to the girl, 'Ask me for anything you want, and I'll give it to you.' And he promised her with an oath, 'Whatever you ask I will give you, up to half my kingdom.' She went out and said to her mother, 'What shall I ask for?' 'The head of John the Baptist,' she answered... The king was greatly distressed, but because of his oaths and his dinner guests, he did not want to refuse her. (NIV)

Reflection

Do you ever get carried away in front of a crowd? Maybe you do so around a meal table by embellishing a story to get a louder laugh from the client you're trying to impress, or by going a bit too far in teasing your friend as you show off your razor-sharp wit. It can be particularly easy to get carried away when we're surrounded by people we want to impress or by those we are intimidated by. Herod was hosting a party for some people he was desperate to win over. 'Act in haste, repent at leisure', or so the saying goes.

And so it is here. In his desperation, Herod makes a fool of himself, promising 'anything' to the daughter of a woman who holds a serious grudge. When the answer comes back, Herod is 'greatly distressed' – and the word here is used in only one other place in Mark's gospel: to describe Jesus in the garden of Gethsemane. Such is the depth of Herod's grief and remorse.

We, too, can find ourselves eating and drinking with people who we want – or feel that we need – to win over, and it is tempting to say or do foolish things in the face of such pressure. Herod's rash promises – and their dire consequences – remind us of the danger of grandiose promises and thoughtless decisions, and the need to use our mealtimes, words and power wisely, even when we fear the judgement of others.

> Father, give me the humility to admit when I am wrong, even in front of those I long to impress.

| Nell Goddard

Great expectations?

Luke 7:31–34

> J esus went on to say, 'To what, then, can I compare the people of this generation? What are they like? They are like children sitting in the market-place and calling out to each other: "We played the pipe for you, and you did not dance; we sang a dirge, and you did not cry." For John the Baptist came neither eating bread nor drinking wine, and you say, "He has a demon." The Son of Man came eating and drinking, and you say, "Here is a glutton and a drunkard, a friend of tax collectors and sinners."' (NIV)

| Nell Goddard

Reflection

'You're not what we expected!' Have you ever been on the receiving end of such a statement?

That was the cry that Jesus was met with throughout his life. People expected the Messiah to come to overthrow the Roman powers, judge the unrighteous and lead his people to victory. Jesus, however, came as a baby, and he spent his time healing the sick, raising the dead and eating with those the religious leaders considered to be the 'wrong' type of people.

And people couldn't cope. Although some believed, many rejected both John the Baptist and Jesus, despite their differing approaches: John preached repentance and led an ascetic life. Jesus led a more 'normal' life but associated and ate with the 'wrong' people. Both were rejected. People did not know what they wanted, and so they couldn't be satisfied.

Is Jesus what you expected? The more time we spend in the gospels, the more likely we are to discover that he isn't... and following him may end up being more challenging than we had anticipated. He doesn't bring condemnation and judgement. He eats with the outcasts, the unclean, the 'sinners'. The ones we might struggle to welcome even into our churches. He sits and eats with them, and he asks us to do the same.

'You're not what we expected!' You can say that in two ways, can't you? In classic disapproval, as you write someone off, or in awe, as you realise that they might not be what you expected, but they're far greater than you could ever have imagined.

> Thank you, Lord, that although you may not be what we expected, you're all we've ever needed. Show me with whom you would have me eat.

Being vs. doing

Luke 10:38–42

As Jesus and his disciples were on their way, he came to a village where a woman named Martha opened her home to him. She had a sister called Mary, who sat at the Lord's feet listening to what he said. But Martha was distracted by all the preparations that had to be made. She came to him and asked, 'Lord, don't you care that my sister has left me to do the work by myself? Tell her to help me!' 'Martha, Martha,' the Lord answered, 'you are worried and upset about many things, but few things are needed – or indeed only one. Mary has chosen what is better, and it will not be taken away from her.' (NIV)

| Nell Goddard

Reflection

Have you ever been to a party where the host was so concerned with everything being perfect that they forgot to spend quality time with you? Or maybe you've been the one hosting and made such a mistake?

In this story Martha, rushed off her feet, is trying to make everything perfect. You can picture her, can't you? Flustered and hot, bustling around while shooting killer glances at her sister Mary, who sits quietly at Jesus' feet, learning and completely oblivious to the fact that Martha is drowning under the weight of her to-do list.

Eventually, Martha cracks and complains about her sister's laziness, but Jesus does not do what she expects. With love, affection, kindness, he chides her: 'Martha, Martha.' His tone is gentle. Mary is the one who has chosen wisely – she has sat at his feet, spent time with him, learnt from him. Jesus does not seem to care whether things around him are in order; he longs only to spend time with his friends: 'Few things are needed – or indeed, only one.'

Where in your life are you flustered, bustling around to make things 'perfect' for God or for those who have come to visit or eat with you? This passage shows us that God does not long for perfectly ordered lives. Instead, he says tenderly to us: 'Few things are needed – or indeed only one.' Today, choose what is better – for it will not be taken away from you.

> Father, help me to stop 'doing' and start 'being'
> in your presence. Help me to be attentive to those
> with whom I eat, too.

Nell Goddard

Family dinner

Luke 14:12–14

Then Jesus said to his host, 'When you give a luncheon or dinner, do not invite your friends, your brothers or sisters, your relatives, or your rich neighbours; if you do, they may invite you back and so you will be repaid. But when you give a banquet, invite the poor, the crippled, the lame, the blind, and you will be blessed. Although they cannot repay you, you will be repaid at the resurrection of the righteous.'

(NIV)

| Nell Goddard

Reflection

Would you charge your family for Christmas lunch? That was the debate sparked by a BBC News article in November 2018. Apparently, the cost of all the festive food and drink plus the stress of cooking for so many has led some people to ask relatives to pay for their Christmas Day meal.

It seems a bit extreme, right? Well, whether that idea fills you with entrepreneurial glee or abject horror, this passage in Luke takes the idea of charging people to attend a meal in your house and pushes it to the other extreme: don't just invite those who *could* pay if you asked them to. Don't even invite those who can bring a contribution. Invite those who can't repay you in any way.

Jesus doesn't couch this instruction in a parable; he isn't being cryptic here: what he says is what he means. Invite to dinner those who cannot pay you back. Open your doors wide to those the world has shut out.

What does that look like? Messy, probably. When I was growing up, we did Christmas dinner like this: anyone at church who would otherwise be alone was free to join us – no charge. One year two guests had a fist fight. Another year someone arrived drunk, ate four mouthfuls, and then vomited all over himself. It wasn't always merry and bright. But I'll never forget the year when one of our guests put his arms around my mum, tears in his eyes, and said quite simply, 'I've spent the last 20 years alone at Christmas. This year, you've reminded me what family looks like, and how it feels to be loved.'

'Invite the poor… and you will be blessed.' Who could you invite to your home or church to dine with you?

> Father, help me to give without wanting or expecting anything in return.

| Nell Goddard

An open invitation

Luke 14:16–18, 21 (abridged)

> Jesus replied: 'A certain man was preparing a great banquet and invited many guests. At the time of the banquet he sent his servant to tell those who had been invited, "Come, for everything is now ready." But they all alike began to make excuses... The servant came back and reported this to his master. Then the owner of the house became angry and ordered his servant, 'Go out quickly into the streets and alleys of the town and bring in the poor, the crippled, the blind and the lame.' (NIV)

| Nell Goddard

Reflection

Have you ever been let down at the last minute? In a world of Facebook 'maybe' responses to invites, it seems to happen all too often. What do you do when you've cooked for 25 and only seven show up? Rearrange the party? Throw the leftovers away? Give everyone boxes full of food to take home?

Would you ever go out into the street and just find whoever you could, invite them in and feed them alongside those you originally invited? That's what the man in this story does.

But this isn't just a story. This is a parable about the kingdom of God. 'Come, for everything is ready,' says God to the Jewish nation. But they make excuses – they're too busy, too distracted, too unprepared. So, instead of cancelling the party, God changes the guest list: now everyone is invited. More specifically, the invitation includes those who are considered 'unclean': the sinners, the broken, the downtrodden, the forgotten.

Here, Jesus is teaching that the kingdom of God is available to all – 'deserving' or not. An exclusive invite has been thrown open to welcome all, for those who were initially invited have made their excuses and gone elsewhere.

In this story, it is we who are the undeserving. We are the broken, the ones who could never repay, and we have been welcomed into the biggest feast imaginable, free of charge. And we have the opportunity to invite others too; for the master wants his house to be full.

Thank you, Father, that you have welcomed me in to your great heavenly banquet. Please show me who else I can invite to join in.

| Nell Goddard

Sibling rivalry

Luke 15:28–32

'"The elder brother became angry and refused to go in. So his father went out and pleaded with him. But he answered his father, "Look! All these years I've been slaving for you and never disobeyed your orders. Yet you never gave me even a young goat so I could celebrate with my friends. But when this son of yours who has squandered your property with prostitutes comes home, you kill the fattened calf for him!" "My son," the father said, "you are always with me, and everything I have is yours. But we had to celebrate and be glad, because this brother of yours was dead and is alive again; he was lost and is found."'

(NIV)

| Nell Goddard

Reflection

There's something about siblings, isn't there? No matter how hard to you try, they have the ability to wind you up like no one else. They always seem to know how to push your buttons and can elicit strong emotions at the drop of a hat.

I think there's a reason Jesus chose to use a sibling relationship to illustrate his point. Many of us who have siblings can no doubt identify – at least in part – with the older brother's strong reaction. He feels cheated. He has worked hard, keeping the rules, while his brother has been out partying and spending money. Now the brother is home, and his father is celebrating? How dare he! This is clear favouritism, and it's directed towards the wrong brother.

Except the elder brother has got it wrong. He's been viewing his father's love as a zero-sum game, assuming that if his brother wins, he loses. If the brother gets more love, it must mean he gets less.

He couldn't be more wrong. His father loves him just the same and invites him into the party as well. Here, Jesus is making the point that although he eats with tax collectors and sinners, welcoming them into the kingdom of God, that does not mean there is no room for those Pharisees who have been tied to the law for so long. God's kingdom is open to any who will accept the invitation – tax collectors and Pharisees alike. There's enough love to go around.

> Thank you, Father, that your love is not a zero-sum game.
> May I demonstrate this with those with whom I eat,
> live and work.

| Inderjit Bhogal

The healing power of eating together

Luke 19:2–7

A man was there named Zacchaeus; he was a chief tax-collector and was rich. He was trying to see who Jesus was, but on account of the crowd he could not, because he was short in stature. So he ran ahead and climbed a sycomore tree to see him, because he was going to pass that way. When Jesus came to the place, he looked up and said to him, 'Zacchaeus, hurry and come down; for I must stay at your house today.' So he hurried down and was happy to welcome him. All who saw it began to grumble and said, 'He has gone to be the guest of one who is a sinner.'

(NRSV)

Reflection

Holy habits can be unpopular and lead to grumbling, opposition and open hostility. This is a frequent event in biblical witness and is often centred around the sharing of food and drink, as in this passage. What is it about the sharing of food and drink that it can arouse hostility?

Often it centres on the elements of food or drink in question or on who is at the table. What is available and who is it being shared with? Many of us are familiar with the situation.

Jesus liked to share food. His habit of sharing food was his most recognisable feature. Who he ate with was a regular criticism, and it got him into trouble.

We see this here in his encounter with Zacchaeus, a little man with a large presence who was not well liked because he collaborated with the occupying Romans and was as a prominent tax collector. Jesus treats Zacchaeus with respect and invites himself to his house for a meal. The murmuring begins because locally Zacchaeus is described as a 'sinner'.

Jesus asks Zacchaeus for hospitality. While others grumble about this, Zacchaeus is happy, and he feels such inclusion and honour that without instruction he changes his ethics from greed to grace and generosity as 'fruits worthy of repentance' (Luke 3:8). Jesus pronounces this as 'salvation' (19:9). Choosing to eat with others, especially those who are generally excluded in community, can inspire generosity and heal relationships.

> What is it about the sharing of food and drink that it can arouse hostility? With whom could you eat to heal a relationship?

73

| Inderjit Bhogal

Eating together – a sign of the kingdom

John 2:7–11

Jesus said to [the servants], 'Fill the jars with water.' And they filled them up to the brim. He said to them, 'Now draw some out, and take it to the chief steward.' So they took it. When the steward tasted the water that had become wine, and did not know where it came from (though the servants who had drawn the water knew), the steward called the bridegroom and said to him, 'Everyone serves the good wine first, and then the inferior wine after the guests have become drunk. But you have kept the good wine until now.' Jesus did this, the first of his signs, in Cana of Galilee, and revealed his glory; and his disciples believed in him.

(NRSV)

| Inderjit Bhogal

Reflection

This significant event took place in Cana, an obscure and sparsely populated place known to us for little else except that Nathaniel came from here (21:2). Jesus may also have regarded Cana as a place for respite (4:46).

In this celebration, Jesus lays down a marker for his disciples. A wedding is taking place. Jesus and his disciples are invited. His mother is there, and possibly his brothers too. Like most African or Asian weddings, the feast will have lasted several days. It is not unusual to run out of supplies and to require more. Jesus is persuaded by his mother to deal with the situation. 'Do whatever he tells you', she commands the stewards (2:5). Jesus changes ordinary water into the best wine. It is like an act of new creation. And as God declares creation as 'good' (Genesis 1), so those who drink the wine pronounce it 'good'. The rejoicing at the wedding is deepened.

It is in the context of a marriage feast that Jesus' disciples have the first insight into his ministry. The most significant thing that happens at this wedding is that 'his disciples believed in him'. No moralism or message drawn; the miracle is just seen as the first of his signs – ministry and the kingdom of God – about eating and celebration and joy, bringing the 'Wow, this is so good' factor into all things. Life and work can be a sign of the kingdom of God.

> We often pray, 'Thy kingdom come.' How might sharing a meal with a colleague, neighbour or stranger be a sign of the kingdom?

Inderjit Bhogal

Intimate eating
John 6:30–35

So they said to [Jesus], 'What sign are you going to give us then, so that we may see it and believe you? What work are you performing? Our ancestors ate the manna in the wilderness; as it is written, "He gave them bread from heaven to eat."' Then Jesus said to them, 'Very truly, I tell you, it was not Moses who gave you the bread from heaven, but it is my Father who gives you the true bread from heaven. For the bread of God is that which comes down from heaven and gives life to the world.' They said to him, 'Sir, give us this bread always.' Jesus said to them, 'I am the bread of life. Whoever comes to me will never be hungry, and whoever believes in me will never be thirsty.' (NRSV)

| Inderjit Bhogal

Reflection

The words of this passage follow the story of Jesus feeding the multitude on a hill with bread and fish (6:1–15), by all accounts a miracle. Now, Jesus is aware the people are only following him because of his miracles. Some are still asking for a sign, 'so that we may see it and believe you'. They remember 'manna in the wilderness', food that was miraculously provided by God for the Israelites on their journey from Egypt.

Jesus uses the experience of having eaten together to open up reflections on what it is to be in relationship with him. He acknowledges that manna was provided by God, but Jesus desires and offers more than good food and good fortune for people. God and Christ insist 'one does not live by bread alone' (Matthew 4:4) and see the word of God as food that nurtures and nourishes the soul.

Here, Jesus is seen as the 'bread of God' who gives 'life to the world'. Jesus says, 'I am the bread of life. Whoever comes to me will never be hungry.' This food and drink supplied endlessly is a symbol of 'grace upon grace' (1:16). It draws the prayer, 'Give us this bread always', and proclaims the mystery that to feed on this bread of life is to eat food that endures forever (6:27, 51) and to abide in him (6:56).

Jesus offers closeness. Intimacy with him is especially deepened through the breaking of bread, another of the holy habits and one that can be practised in the context of eating together.

> At a meal time today, take time to craft a new prayer of grace, asking that your intimacy with Jesus may be deepened as you eat.

| Inderjit Bhogal

Sacred meals

John 21:9–13

When [the disciples] had gone ashore, they saw a charcoal fire there, with fish on it, and bread. Jesus said to them, 'Bring some of the fish that you have just caught.' So Simon Peter went aboard and hauled the net ashore, full of large fish, a hundred and fifty-three of them; and though there were so many, the net was not torn. Jesus said to them, 'Come and have breakfast.' Now none of the disciples dared to ask him, 'Who are you?' because they knew it was the Lord. Jesus came and took the bread and gave it to them, and did the same with the fish. (NRSV)

Reflection

Picture the scene: a beach, early morning, just after daybreak. A group of men are fishing out in the water. A man has a charcoal fire burning on the sand. He has a handful of fish on the fire for a breakfast barbecue on the beach. The man calls out to the fishermen, instructing them where to cast the net. They follow his call and suddenly the net is full to bursting. Who is he?

Suddenly, one of the fishermen recognises Jesus. What gives him away? His wisdom and knowledge of fish? That he is preparing food?

Peter appears to be a little embarrassed. The last time he was near a charcoal fire (18:18), he denied he was a friend of Jesus. Jesus invites the men to bring some of their fish, and Peter fetches them. Then we hear Jesus' lovely invitation: 'Come and have breakfast.'

A familiar action follows. Jesus is host: he 'took the bread and gave it to them, and did the same with the fish'. The last meal of bread and fish is recorded in John 6:1–14, when a boy offers five loaves and two fish, and a multitude are fed. Now, Jesus provides some bread and fish, and Peter fetches the large haul of fish.

Jesus' action as host is eucharistic. It is full of grace and thanksgiving, as were all the meals Jesus shared, in a variety of places – at a wedding, by a well, on a hillside, in a home, in an upper room, on a beach – with a variety of people – women and men and children. No one is excluded, not even those who deny or betray him. These meals are a foretaste of the kingdom.

Lord, as I eat today, may it be a sacred act and may I be nourished to be a means of grace to others.

Inderjit Bhogal

Broadened horizons

Acts 10:11–16, 19–20

[Peter] saw the heaven opened and something like a large sheet coming down, being lowered to the ground by its four corners. In it were all kinds of four-footed creatures and reptiles and birds of the air. Then he heard a voice saying, 'Get up, Peter; kill and eat.' But Peter said, 'By no means, Lord; for I have never eaten anything that is profane or unclean.' The voice said to him again, a second time, 'What God has made clean, you must not call profane.' This happened three times, and the thing was suddenly taken up to heaven... While Peter was still thinking about the vision, the Spirit said to him, 'Look, three men are searching for you. Now get up, go down, and go with them without hesitation; for I have sent them.'

(NRSV)

| Inderjit Bhogal

Reflection

Peter took some persuading. His response to new insight was often a clear 'no'. Three times he denies he is a friend of Jesus; three times he is asked to affirm his discipleship; three times he is taught a lesson about God's impartiality.

In Joppa, Jonah turned his back on God's mission and bigger vision. In Joppa, too, Peter initially said 'no' to God's call to impartiality and inclusion. Peter's conversion was aided by his encounter with Cornelius, a prayerful, influential but no doubt despised Italian soldier.

Cornelius and Peter had never met, but each had a vision at around the same time. In Cornelius' vision, God called him by name and assured him that his prayers were heard. What Cornelius' prayer was, we don't know. We do know he was asked to send for Peter.

Peter's vision occurs three times. Peter was still puzzling over its meaning when his three visitors suddenly appeared. Peter invited these three strangers in and offered them overnight hospitality. Perhaps it was during this time that the meaning of his vision began to take shape, achieving clarity the next day through his meeting with Cornelius, another stranger. Food was used to teach Peter that there are no 'profane or unclean' people, and that 'God shows no partiality' (10:34).

In sharing hospitality and kindness to strangers Peter found he was entertaining people sent by God, and this reluctant learner had his understanding of God broadened.

> With whom might you share hospitality and kindness today? Be alert to God's promptings as you go about your business.

| Inderjit Bhogal

Body building

Romans 14:14–19

> I know and am persuaded in the Lord Jesus that nothing is unclean in itself; but it is unclean for anyone who thinks it unclean. If your brother or sister is being injured by what you eat, you are no longer walking in love. Do not let what you eat cause the ruin of one for whom Christ died. So do not let your good be spoken of as evil. For the kingdom of God is not food and drink but righteousness and peace and joy in the Holy Spirit. The one who thus serves Christ is acceptable to God and has human approval. Let us then pursue what makes for peace and for mutual edification.
>
> (NRSV)

| Inderjit Bhogal

Reflection

There is diversity in all congregations. Here, some members of the congregation are described as 'weak' (14:1) and some as 'strong' (15:1). Some were new and others were mature in faith, and there were differences of opinion. One of the controversies in the newly forming church communities was around 'clean' and 'unclean' food, and we have an insight into it here.

Peter wrestled with this issue (Acts 10; Galatians 2:11–15). For Jesus (Mark 7:15; Matthew 15:11), the issue was not so much what goes into your mouth (food) as what comes out of it (thought and language).

It was important to be considerate towards each other and of differences of opinion and to walk in love. Given the situation, it was incumbent upon all members to cultivate peace. What would demonstrate this aim? Mutual edification. This required each individual to be 'fully convinced in their own minds' (14:5) that others were not 'injured by' their actions or words and that they did not 'cause the ruin of one for whom Christ died'.

The term 'mutual edification' is a reminder that the church is the body of Christ and that each member is also the temple of God. Do everything for the edification of the body: use words and actions that are nourishing; act in ways that build up, not tear up, the body; be constructive not destructive; pay attention to the views of all, especially those who may feel undermined in their faith. This is what serves Christ, makes for peace and builds the kingdom of God.

> How could you eat together in your church, or with other churches, as a way of helping to build up the body of Christ?

Thoughtful eating

1 Corinthians 10:24–31

Do not seek your own advantage, but that of others. Eat whatever is sold in the meat market without raising any question on the ground of conscience, for 'the earth and its fullness are the Lord's.' If an unbeliever invites you to a meal and you are disposed to go, eat whatever is set before you without raising any question on the ground of conscience. But if someone says to you, 'This has been offered in sacrifice', then do not eat it, out of consideration for the one who informed you, and for the sake of conscience – I mean the other's conscience, not your own. For why should my liberty be subject to the judgement of someone else's conscience? If I partake with thankfulness, why should I be denounced because of that for which I give thanks? So, whether you eat or drink, or whatever you do, do everything for the glory of God.

(NRSV)

Reflection

The theme of mutuality and thoughtful consideration for others continues in this passage. The words preceding this passage, 'Consider the people of Israel' (10:18), remind us that the context is interfaith.

The earliest Christian communities faced differences of opinion, especially around food, between those of Jewish or Gentile backgrounds. There would also have been issues between those who could afford to buy and eat meat regularly and those who perhaps could only afford to eat meat at public events where it may also have been offered in sacrifice. There were theological differences, too, between those who held no qualms about food and quoted scripture, stating, 'The earth and its fullness are the Lord's', and those who as a matter of 'conscience' would not eat food offered in sacrifice.

These matters are important today in Christian communities around the world and an important consideration in interfaith meetings and dialogue. Christians from Buddhist, Hindu, Jain, Jewish, Islamic, Sikh or Zoroastrian backgrounds may raise questions about the consumption of meat, especially beef or pork, and about halal or kosher food, not least because of rites and prayers involved in food preparation. 'Meat or veg?' is a routine question and conversation in meals.

In diverse and complex communities, 2,000 years ago and now, the consideration of different needs and views is essential. The aim remains for behaviour that will 'build up' relationships and communities (10:23), to avoid actions that 'seek your own advantage' and to seek only the glory of God.

> Lord, grant me wisdom and sensitivity in the food that I choose and the food that I share.

Eating together

1 Corinthians 11:17–22

Now in the following instructions I do not commend you, because when you come together it is not for the better but for the worse. For, to begin with, when you come together as a church, I hear that there are divisions among you; and to some extent I believe it. Indeed, there have to be factions among you, for only so will it become clear who among you are genuine. When you come together, it is not really to eat the Lord's supper. For when the time comes to eat, each of you goes ahead with your own supper, and one goes hungry and another becomes drunk. What! Do you not have homes to eat and drink in? Or do you show contempt for the church of God and humiliate those who have nothing? What should I say to you? Should I commend you? In this matter I do not commend you! (NRSV)

Reflection

This chapter contains the only account of the institution of the Lord's supper outside the gospels. This account includes some reflections on what actually seems to take place at the gatherings for the Lord's supper.

The act, which should help the followers of Christ to 'come together' and build the body of Christ, appears to be making relationships worse. The picture that emerges is that of divisions and factions, reflected at a meal between those who had homes and could afford to eat there and those who were not in this position. The evidence for this also includes selfish behaviour, each member eating their own supper, which meant that some ate or drank more than others, resulting in some going hungry and others getting drunk. Those who arrived first or were hungry did not wait for others. The unifying act had become a divisive act. It had become a sphere of gluttony rather than a means of grace.

This behaviour is destructive rather than edifying and not worthy of either the Lord's supper or any other shared meal. Later, Paul gives the instruction to wait for the whole assembly to gather before the eating commences and to treat each other equally at the table (11:33).

> Lord, forgive us when our selfishness and greed damages or degrades others. Help us to recover a sense of the sacredness of eating together.

| Inderjit Bhogal

Holiness reflected in thankfulness

1 Timothy 4:1–5

Now the Spirit expressly says that in later times some will renounce the faith by paying attention to deceitful spirits and teachings of demons, through the hypocrisy of liars whose consciences are seared with a hot iron. They forbid marriage and demand abstinence from foods, which God created to be received with thanksgiving by those who believe and know the truth. For everything created by God is good, and nothing is to be rejected, provided it is received with thanksgiving; for it is sanctified by God's word and by prayer.   (NRSV)

Reflection

Christian diversity includes single, celibate and married people, and also vegetarians, vegans and omnivores. Some people are in loving relationships without marriage. Some fast or abstain from certain foods at particular times; others don't. Asceticism is not holier or more spiritual than participation. It is easy to see our own lifestyle as holy and the standard for others or to regard some lifestyles as dirty, particularly in matters relating to food. Jesus cautioned against this (Mark 7:18–19).

The few words of this passage suggest a discussion, and there is a hint that some people may have seen items of food shared in the Lord's supper as unholy or unclean, bearing in mind that in the earliest Christian communities this holy sacrament was a full meal. There appears also to be a discussion between believers and non-believers.

The wisdom of the text cautions against hypocrisy, reminding readers that 'everything created by God is good', recalling the words of Genesis 1:31, and is not to be seen as 'unclean' (Acts 10:15, 28; 11:9). An appropriate way to share in human relationships and food is to receive, not reject, and give thanks for people in your life and for food. They are gifts of God, nourishing and edifying. Holiness is reflected in thankfulness.

Believers and non-believers can be thankful; this is not a quality that is the preserve of any one type of people. What deepens the holiness of any action and makes sacrament complete is that all things are 'sanctified by God's word and by prayer'.

Before you eat in the evening, take a little time to give thanks, not just for the food and drink before you but also for all the other blessings you have received today.

Inderjit Bhogal

An open door, an open heart and an open table

Revelation 3:18–22

'Therefore I counsel you to buy from me gold refined by fire so that you may be rich; and white robes to clothe you and to keep the shame of your nakedness from being seen; and salve to anoint your eyes so that you may see. I reprove and discipline those whom I love. Be earnest, therefore, and repent. Listen! I am standing at the door, knocking; if you hear my voice and open the door, I will come in to you and eat with you, and you with me. To the one who conquers I will give a place with me on my throne, just as I myself conquered and sat down with my Father on his throne. Let anyone who has an ear listen to what the Spirit is saying to the churches.' (NRSV)

| Inderjit Bhogal

Reflection

This passage contains one of the most familiar verses and images in the New Testament, portrayed in Holman Hunt's *The Light of the World*. In the famous painting, Christ is shown standing and knocking at a door, eager for it to open so that he can enter in and build warm relationships. The context here is Christ's challenge to the lukewarm church of Laodicea.

Readers have interpreted this passage as Christ knocking on the door of the heart (personal) or church generally (social) and as a symbol of evangelistic preaching. There are other ways some interpret this. For example, Christ could be seen as a refugee who has been knocking on the door for a long time, hoping it will open. In Hunt's painting, the door is firmly shut and has been for a long time, as seen from the rusty hinges and overgrown briers.

The light of God revealed in Christ illuminates all people (John 1:9). 'If you hear my voice and open the door' refers to all humanity. There is a universal challenge and invitation here. The voice is made audible in the knock of the figure at the door. This is not just a spoken voice. There is a need to discern the voice of Christ in promptings and knocking around us and in our experiences. Opening the door is essential to building community. Hospitality is the doorway to refreshing, nurturing, mutually enriching relationships.

To whom is Christ calling you to open the door and share a meal with? Might it be a colleague at work at lunchtime, an elderly neighbour or the *Big Issue* seller at the station?

Whole-church resources

Individual copy £4.99

Holy Habits is an adventure in Christian discipleship. Inspired by Luke's model of church found in Acts 2:42–47, it identifies ten habits and encourages the development of a way of life formed by them. These resources are designed to help churches explore the habits creatively in a range of contexts and live them out in whole-life, intergenerational, missional discipleship.

MISSIONAL DISCIPLESHIP RESOURCES FOR CHURCHES

HOLY**HABITS**

Group Studies

Edited by Andrew Roberts
Individual copy £6.99

These new additions to the Holy Habits resources have been developed to help church groups explore the Holy Habits through prayerful engagement with the Bible and live them out in whole-life, missional discipleship.

Each leader's guide contains eight sessions of Bible study material, providing off-the-peg material to help churches get started or continue with Holy Habits. Each session includes a Bible passage, reflection, group questions, community/outreach ideas, art and media links and a prayer.

Other Bible Reflections currently available:

Edited by Andrew Roberts
Individual copy £3.99

Group Studies and Bible Reflections for the remaining five habits
BREAKING BREAD | SHARING RESOURCES | SERVING | GLADNESS AND GENEROSITY | WORSHIP will be available in February 2020.

Find out more at holyhabits.org.uk
and brfonline.org.uk/collections/holy-habits
Download a leaflet for your church leadership at
brfonline.org.uk/holyhabitsdownload

Are you looking to continue the habit of daily Bible reading?

With a subscription to BRF Bible reading notes, you'll have everything you need to nourish your relationship with the Bible and with God.

Our most popular and longest running series, *New Daylight*, features daily readings and reflections from a selection of much-beloved writers, dealing with a variety of themes and Bible passages. With the relevant passage printed alongside the comment, *New Daylight* is a practical and effective way of reading the Bible as a part of your everyday routine.

New Daylight is available in print, deluxe (large print), by email and as an app for iOS and Android.

'I think Bible reading notes are really underrated. At any age – there I was as a teenager getting as much out of them then as I am now – so they're for every age group, not just the very young and the very old. I think to have them as your bedside companion is a really wise idea throughout life.'
Debbie Thrower, Pioneer of BRF's Anna Chaplaincy programme

MAY–AUGUST 2019

BRF

New Daylight

Sustaining your daily journey with the Bible

Included in this issue
Harvest PAUL GRAVELLE
Judges 1—12 AMY BOUCHER PYE
Resilience TONY HORSFALL

Also available:

Find out more at brfonline.org.uk

Praise for the original Holy Habits resources

'Here are some varied and rich resources to help further deepen our discipleship of Christ, encouraging and enabling us to adopt the life-transforming habits that make for following Jesus.'
Revd Dr Martyn Atkins, Team Leader & Superintendent Minister, Methodist Central Hall, Westminster

'The Holy Habits resources will help you, your church, your fellowship group, to engage in a journey of discovery about what it really means to be a disciple today. I know you will be encouraged, challenged and inspired as you read and work your way through… There is lots to study together and pray about, and that can only be good as our churches today seek to bring about the kingdom of God.'
Revd Loraine Mellor, President of the Methodist Conference 2017/18

'The Holy Habits resources help weave the spiritual through everyday life. They're a great tool that just get better with use. They help us grow in our desire to follow Jesus as their concern is formation not simply information.'
Olive Fleming Drane and John Drane

'The Holy Habits resources are an insightful and comprehensive manual for living in the way of Jesus in the 21st century: an imaginative, faithful and practical gift for the church that will sustain and invigorate our life and mission in a demanding world. The Holy Habits resources are potentially transformational for a church.'
Revd Ian Adams, Mission Spirituality Adviser for Church Mission Society

'To understand the disciplines of the Christian life without practising them habitually is like owning a fine collection of soap but never having a wash. The team behind Holy Habits knows this, which is why they have produced these excellent and practical resources. Use them, and by God's grace you will grow in holiness.'
Paul Bayes, Bishop of Liverpool